Unleased Potential: Mastering Life's Crucial Skills for Career Triumph

Derek D. Bussan

DEDICATION

This book is especially dedicated to my dear dog, **_Hope_**, a faithful companion throughout the last 12 years of my career journey, whose recent passing has left a profound void. Her steadfast presence was a source of comfort and inspiration along my path.

TABLE OF CONTENTS

ACKNOWLEDGMENTS

I extend my deepest gratitude to my family, whose constant support and love have been the bedrock of my journey. Additionally, I am immensely thankful for the encouragement bestowed upon me by friends and colleagues. It is through their faith and belief in me that I have reached a point where writing this book has become possible.

CHAPTER 1 PRELUDE: FOUNDATIONS OF INSPIRATION

Unleashed Potential: Mastering Life's Crucial Skills for Career Triumph

Thank you for choosing this book! I'm grateful for the opportunity to share the insights I've gained from various facets of my life, including work, education, extracurricular activities, and relationships with family, friends, and even pets. This book, written in 2023, represents my endeavor to encapsulate these valuable experiences and provide you with relevant and practical guidance. As this is the first edition, I plan to update it every five to seven years to keep pace with technological advancements, ensuring that its contents remain timely and beneficial for the foreseeable future.

Background about myself

I have devoted over 20 years of my adult life to higher education. My journey began at the University of Iowa, where I earned a BA in Chemistry and a minor in Math. This was followed by a Master of Science in Inorganic Chemistry from Oklahoma State University. My next step led me to Oxford, MS, where I completed my Ph.D. in Chemistry, a degree I once thought would be my last. However, I soon realized that learning is a lifelong endeavor, leading me to later pursue an MBA at Eastern Kentucky University while teaching there.

My career has spanned universities, private industry, and the federal government. With these varied experiences, I now feel compelled to give back to the community that has enriched me and to share my knowledge and expertise. The most important lesson I've learned is the importance of doing something you love, while also ensuring that it provides a decent compensation package, opportunities for career advancement, and a healthy work-life balance.

This book offers insights into subjects and knowledge that are not typically emphasized in academic settings—at least, they weren't during my time as a student. I don't fault my past instructors, as they had limited time to cover the necessary material. Now, I understand that perhaps they didn't know about or only had limited knowledge of the topics presented in this book. I hope you find this book enjoyable and informative. And as always, if you have any questions, comments, or remarks, please feel free to add me on LinkedIn. I would love to connect and hear from you!

Purpose of This Book

This guide is primarily tailored for individuals living in the United States, though many skills and insights may be universally applicable. My diverse experiences in industry, federal work, and academia uniquely position me to advise students aspiring to enter STEM, business, or any other field. In truth, every career path is intertwined with business principles. The ultimate goal? To secure resources for a fulfilling, comfortable life – this definition has multiple meanings and interpretations and depends on your end goal. My end goal for a career was always to try to find fulfilling work both mentally and financially.

Addressing the Education Gap

As many readers who are not chemistry majors might appreciate, the following example, while focused on chemistry, highlights a broader issue in education. Consider the teaching of the Diels-Alder reaction in a typical organic chemistry course. This reaction, while a fundamental concept in the field, is often presented in a purely academic context. Its significant industrial applications, such as in the production of Vitamin B-6 – a market that is projected to reach in the millions of USD – are rarely mentioned. This is not unique to chemistry; across various disciplines, there is a noticeable gap in linking academic concepts to their practical, financial applications.

In many educational settings, the focus remains predominantly on theoretical knowledge, with little emphasis on how this knowledge translates into tangible economic value. For instance, in economics classes, the practical aspects of personal finance, investment strategies, or the implications of economic policies on individual finances might not be adequately covered. Similarly, in technology and engineering courses, while students learn the principles and technical skills, the entrepreneurial and market aspects of these skills are often not emphasized.

This gap in education means that students are frequently left unprepared to understand and leverage the real-world, financial implications of their studies. As a result, there is a lack of financial literacy among graduates, who might be academically proficient but are unaware of the economic potential and career opportunities associated with their fields of study.

Moreover, this oversight in education can lead to a disconnect between academic pursuits and career choices. Students might choose or discard fields of study based on perceived financial prospects, which are not always clearly communicated or understood. This lack of practical financial education also means graduates are often ill-equipped to make informed decisions about their career paths, investments, and financial planning.

Addressing this issue requires a more integrated approach to education, where alongside academic theory, the financial and practical applications of the subject matter are also discussed. This can include case studies, industry collaborations, guest lectures from professionals, and coursework that ties academic concepts to real-world financial outcomes. Such an approach would not only enhance the relevance of the education but also empower students with a more comprehensive understanding of how their knowledge can be applied in a financially rewarding manner.

This book aims to bridge the significant oversight in educational settings where real-world considerations and values are often omitted. By addressing this gap, this book seeks to better prepare students for the realities they will face post-graduation, ensuring they are equipped not only with theoretical knowledge but also with a comprehensive understanding of its real-world applications and value.

What This Book Offers

To bridge this educational gap, this book delves into practical aspects not typically covered in academic curriculums but crucial for professional success. It's a guide that fills in essential gaps, preparing students to make informed career decisions. The topics covered included by chapter are:

Chapter 2: Resume Writing

Chapter 3: Job Applications

Chapter 4: Interviewing Techniques

Chapter 5: Identifying Quality Employers

Chapter 6: Essential Skills Beyond School Curriculum

Chapter 7: Student/Instructor Exercises.

This book aims to be one of many resources for students across disciplines, providing insights and tools crucial for navigating the professional world.

Each topic covered in this book represents a crucial skill set, ideally imparted to students during their undergraduate and graduate studies. Unfortunately, the current educational landscape lacks a comprehensive resource that bridges this gap effectively. Standard curricula often miss these practical skills, leaving students underprepared for the professional world that awaits them.

Recognizing this need, I have crafted this book to serve as a versatile and practical handbook. It's designed not just for STEM and business students but for a broad audience spanning various disciplines across the nation. This book aims to fill a significant void in traditional education, offering valuable insights and tools essential for success beyond the classroom.

This book is designed to arm students with essential skills and knowledge for successfully navigating today's complex job market and building rewarding careers. It emphasizes the importance of gainful employment and professional fulfillment. Additionally, Chapter 7 offers practical examples, applicable both in classroom settings and for individual practice, allowing students and instructors to actively engage with and apply the concepts discussed.

CHAPTER 2: CRAFTING AN EFFECTIVE RESUME

The art of resume writing is a pivotal skill in the job application process. Often, it's the first impression you make on a potential employer, serving as a crucial screening tool among numerous applicants. Drawing from my experiences both as a job applicant and a hiring committee chair, I've learned that a great resume isn't about length. It's about impact and clarity.

Below, you'll find my resume as it currently stands in 2023. This resume is not for direct replication; copying it verbatim won't do you any favors in the application process. Instead, view it as a template to guide the structure and content of your own resume. Remember, hiring managers typically spend only 15-20 seconds per resume, given the sheer volume they often have to review. Therefore, your resume should be distinctive, featuring relevant keywords and being succinct yet informative.

A point worth noting while a cover letter is commonly required, it's ultimately the resume that can clinch the interview. A crucial tip for your cover letter: always double-check that you've addressed it to the correct company or institution. It may sound trivial, but a mismatch between the company applied to and the one mentioned in your cover letter can be a deal-breaker. It suggests a lack of attention to detail and seriousness about the specific position, leading your application to be dismissed prematurely.

So, while these errors may seem small, they can have significant implications. Ensure that your resume and cover letter are both tailor-made for the role you're applying for – this level of specificity and attention to detail can make all the difference.

AUTHORS RESUME:

Derek D. Bussan   **PHONE**: 111.222.3333
                                                        E-MAIL:

author@hopemydog.com

ADDRESS: 112233 1st Avenue North
                Somewhere, IA 52001

EDUCATION

MBA, Eastern Kentucky University, 2022
Ph.D., Analytical Chemistry, University of Mississippi, 2015
M.S., Inorganic Chemistry, Oklahoma State University, 2011
B.A., General Chemistry, Minor in Mathematics, University of Iowa, 2004

WORK AND PROFESSIONAL EXPERIENCE

SUPERVISORY/MANAGERIAL COMPETENCIES
Leadership and Team Management:
- Demonstrated ability in leading and accomplishing work through others, with a strong focus on team building and effective conflict management.
- Adept at fostering cultural awareness within teams, promoting an inclusive and collaborative work environment.
- Proficient in strategic thinking and technology management, skillfully integrating innovative solutions to enhance team productivity and project outcomes.
- Politically savvy, with a keen understanding of organizational dynamics, enabling effective navigation through complex situations and decision-making processes.

Communication and Diversity Engagement:
- Exceptional ability in communicating with individuals and groups from diverse backgrounds, ensuring clear and effective dialogue in a variety of situations.
- Experienced in adapting communication styles to suit different audiences, whether in formal presentations, team meetings, or one-on-one interactions.
- Proven track record of successful collaboration and negotiation with multiple stakeholders, including government officials, scientific peers, and industry partners.
- Committed to fostering an environment of mutual respect and understanding, leveraging diversity as a strength in team dynamics and decision-making.

United States Department of Agriculture – 2/23-present Research Chemistry Manager (1320 Chemistry Series– Friday 8:30-5:00pm 40 hours a week)

As an expert resource overseeing the operations of the Nutritional Analytic Laboratory (NAL) as well as budget overseeing a budget of X dollars/year. My role encompasses various responsibilities involving budget preparation, equipment procurement, personnel management, and research oversight.

Effectively negotiated an instrument agreement, achieving a cost reduction from XK to XK, thereby enhancing our laboratory infrastructure.

One of my key responsibilities is to prepare and present the lab's annual budget for each fiscal year, following Generally Accepted Accounting Principles (GAAP). This involves conducting market research and negotiating prices for both service contracts and instrumentation, particularly for large ticket items exceeding XK. Collaborating with the center director, center scientists, lab technicians, and administrative and accounting officers from our center and regional office, I ensure that the budget aligns with the lab's operational needs and strategic objectives.

Additionally, I am actively involved in overseeing sample preparation for laboratory technicians. This includes tasks such as organic extraction, solid phase extraction, or acid digestion for analysis across a complex array of biological matrices, including food samples. By ensuring proper sample preparation techniques, I contribute to the accuracy and reliability of the laboratory's analytical results.

The laboratory is equipped with a diverse range of instruments and equipment, including:
- Three LC-MS systems (SCIEX-5500, SCIEX-6500, and a Shimadzu 8050).
- A brand new ICP-MS – Perkin Elmer Nexion 5000.
- Three Thermo Trace 1310 gas chromatography systems.
- A CEM Sprint protein analyzer, as well as the CEM percent fat and moisture analyzer, and a CEM Blade microwave for mineral digestion.
- A UV-visible spectrometer.
- Multiple -80°C freezers.
- Numerous Peak gas generators, reducing the need for purchasing gas tanks.
- Plus, many more ancillary instruments and equipment to support a wide array of laboratory activities.

In my role as a manager, I also plan and direct research studies. Serving as an investigator, I utilize both sophisticated and standard methods, applying a high degree of originality to advance scientific understanding in the field. I am responsible for developing papers and abstracts based on the data generated from methods development, providing input for manuscripts, and reviewing papers and abstracts from the analyses of studies. This involvement in the scientific community helps disseminate knowledge and contributes to the advancement of nutritional analysis methodologies.

To stay abreast of the latest analytical methodologies, I actively participate in scientific meetings and workshops. These events provide opportunities to exchange ideas with other scientists, learn about emerging techniques, and remain at the forefront of advancements in the field. This knowledge sharing enables me to implement state-of-the-art methodologies and technologies within the laboratory.

In my day-to-day operations, I utilize a range of tools and software applications. These include word processing, spreadsheets, relational databases, email, statistical software packages, and specialized instrumentation and analytical software programs such as R. Proficiency in these tools allows me to efficiently manage data, perform statistical analyses, and generate comprehensive reports.

As a manager, I outline work assignments and provide guidance on procedures and methods to be employed. I review work in progress to ensure quality and adherence to established protocols. Additionally, I identify and implement training courses that enhance the skills of lab personnel and introduce novel methods and equipment to improve the utilization of human, technical, and fiscal resources.

In my role, a significant responsibility includes hiring and evaluating lab personnel, with a pivotal focus on collaborating with union leaders, particularly from the American Federation of Government Employees (AFGE). This collaboration ensures adherence to fair labor practices and union standards. I conduct comprehensive performance reviews, offering constructive feedback and identifying areas for growth, always in alignment with AFGE guidelines. My effective communication and partnership with union leaders play a crucial role in ensuring equitable treatment and fostering a supportive and compliant work environment. By building a capable, motivated team that respects union principles, I not only boost the lab's productivity but also create a positive culture that aligns with the lab's objectives and fosters professional development among staff.

- Managed service contracts by collaborating with manufacturers and third-party vendors to ensure efficient laboratory operations.
- Negotiated and finalized contracts, overseeing the terms and conditions for equipment maintenance and service.
- Facilitated communication between the laboratory and vendors, ensuring timely service and maintenance of equipment.

- Coordinated with internal teams to align service contract requirements with the laboratory's needs, optimizing workflow and productivity.
- Provided support in troubleshooting equipment issues, liaising between technical support and laboratory staff for swift resolutions.

It should also be noted that I serve on two editorial boards as this establishes my credibility within the scientific community.

The MBA has proven a valuable tool as I have gained the necessary communication skills to effectively utilize the use of federal funds to the center's advantage. The funds that I have saved the center can now be utilized for other goods and services.

I also want to point out that I have a great rapport with the people at the center to motivate our technicians and wage-grade employees. This is important as you want to ensure everyone feels appreciated not only because this is the right thing to do, but it also creates a more motivated workforce.

In summary, as the manager overseeing the operations of the Nutritional Analytic Laboratory, my role extends beyond managing the budget and laboratory equipment. I actively contribute to research, scientific collaboration, and personnel development, ensuring the lab operates efficiently and maintains high standards of scientific excellence.

I was the corresponding author on a review paper with Rob Thomas (World Expert in ICP-OES/MS) regarding the fundamentals of ICP, accepted to Science of the Total Environment impact factor: 9.8.

Douvris, Chris, Vaughan Trey, **Derek Bussan**, Georgios Bartzas, and Robert Thomas. "How ICP-OES changed the face of trace element analysis: Review of the global application landscape." *Science of The Total Environment* (2023): 167242.

USDA scientists routinely turn to me for guidance in developing analytical methods across a wide spectrum of sample matrices, encompassing soil, food, plasma, bone, and water. These methods are crafted to analyze a diverse array of substances, including, but not limited to, minerals, carotenoids, vitamin D, cortisol, lipids, fatty acid methyl esters, and various other analytes.

University of North Dakota Nistler College of Business Adjunct Marketing Instructor: August -2023 - present

Dedicated and experienced educator specializing in Business Communications and Negotiations. Proven track record of instructing business students in the art of effective communication strategies and negotiation techniques. Skilled in fostering a dynamic and engaging learning environment that empowers students to excel in their professional communication endeavors. Recognized for leveraging real-world examples and interactive teaching methods to enhance students' practical skills in written, verbal, and intercultural communication, as well as persuasive negotiation tactics.

Eastern Kentucky University - Assistant Professor, Chemistry, 08/19-02/23. 40 hours/week

- Increased enrollment beginning in 2019 from 199 students in the forensics program (FEPAC accredited) to currently 250 students, this represented in increase in revenue of $2.0 million USD to $2.3 million USD, during the same time period I have helped increase summer organic chemistry revenue from $17K to currently $136K.
- Managed and oversaw nine undergraduate research projects.
- Chaired two hiring committees and served on three other committees.
- Voted faculty senator by my fellow peers in my department.
- Over 20 external collaborators including the FDA, Valvoline and Brewing and Distilling analytical services.
- Published seven peer-reviewed articles.
- Invited to contribute to a Springer book titled "The Handbook of Environmental Chemistry, with the topic "Metal(loid)s in the Environment'.
- Brought in over 20 seminar speakers including academic, industry and government speakers.
- Served as an academic advisor to over 100 chemistry and forensics students.
- Served as the Data subcommittee Chair for the Kentucky Telehealth Program.

McNeese State University - Assistant Professor, Chemistry, 08/17-08/19 40 hours/week

- $718,000.00 USD Equipment Enhancement Grant to update existing chemistry instrumentation. This money was used to purchase a GC-MS, ICP-MS, Tabletop NMR, LC-MS and Microlab units.
- Spearheaded the Forensic Chemistry Unit, overseeing the most popular concentration for our chemistry students, which constituted more than 50% of our chemistry program enrollment, comprising 40 students on average at the time.

- Acquired quotes and purchased instruments from various instrument manufacturers for the aforementioned instruments.
- $5,000.00 USD Endowed Professorship award funded in 2018 and 2019.
- Served as Assistant Department Head and Instrument Manager of the Department.
- Lead one masters student thesis project.
- Involved with local industries including Phillips 66, Sasol and the Calcasieu Parishes forensics crime lab in placing students in internships and potential employment opportunities.
- Helped manage six employees as assistant department head, these duties included but not limited to creating and managing schedules, evaluating performance, providing feedback for performance and resolving employee issues and disputes.

Lancaster Eurofins/Altria (40hrs/week) 12 Month Contract

Richmond, VA
Senior Scientist/Post Doc 40hrs/week   **2016 –2017**
- In charge of the trace metals lab at Altria (fortune 200 company.)
- Managed a worldwide interlaboratory metals proficiency study in 2017 for assessing laboratory capabilities for analyzing specific trace elements in tobacco and tobacco products. Proficiency testing is an important component of a quality system and is a requirement of ISO 17025 accreditation.
- *As a senior scientist I lead a team of two PhD chemists, this included method development and daily production output.*
- Helped create standard operating procedures for trace elements in smokeless tobacco products.
- Was able to get a 400K instrument up and running after 8 years of nonuse.
- Presented an oral poster presentation at the 71st Tobacco Science Research Conference in 2017.
- Developed and coordinated biologic, hydrologic, and environmental science projects to meet research and regulatory objectives for the Center of Tobacco Products under the FDA.
- Played a pivotal role in developing and influencing the scientific, administrative, and technical policies, standards, procedures, and instructions required for the effective direction and operation of the trace metals lab.
- Acted as the principal contact with Federal agencies, state and local government organizations, and other stakeholders, ensuring alignment and cooperation for the success of trace metals analysis in tobacco and tobacco products.

Oak Ridge National Laboratory (40hrs/week)   **Oak Ridge, TN**
Post-Doctoral Research Associate   **2015 -2016**
- Developed an analytical method that can separate transition and rare earth elements utilizing HPLC-ICP-MS.
- Presented our research findings to representatives from the Defense Threat Reduction Agency.
- Underwent radioactive worker training for radioactive waste.
- Worked with faculty members from the University of Tennessee on research projects.

PROFESSIONAL MEMBERSHIPS
- American Chemical Society, 2012-present
- Journal of Distilling Science – 2021 -present; Member of the Editorial Board.
- Multidisciplinary Digital Publishing Institute – 2021-present reviewer
- American Society of Nutrition, 2023- present
- Editorial Board Member Biological Trace Element Research – 2023-present

Courses Taught:

University of North Dakota:
- BADM 225: Business Communications

Eastern Kentucky University:
- CHE 111: General Chemistry I
- CHE 325: Quantitative Analysis
- CHE 385W: Chemical Literature
- CHE 361: Organic Chemistry I
- CHE 362: Organic Chemistry II
- CHE 484: Chemistry Colloquium
- CHE 485: Chemistry Seminar
- CHE 501A: Absolute Basics of ICP-MS & ICP-OES
- CHE 520: Mass Spectrometry
- CHE 701A: Absolute Basics of ICP-MS & ICP-OES - Graduate Students
- CHE 720: Mass Spectrometry - Graduate Students
- CHE 810: Professional Training
- CHE 880: Graduate Seminar
- CHE 881: Graduate Colloquium
- FOR 451: Forensic Microscopy
- FOR 465W: Expert Witness Testimony

McNeese State University:
- General Chemistry I
- General Chemistry II
- Quantitative Analysis
- Instrumental Analysis
- Forensic Chemistry
- Organic Chemistry I
- Organic Chemistry II

AWARDS AND PUBLICATIONS

Teaching: Pinnacle Award, 2018- McNeese State University
Publications: 15 peer reviewed publications

1. Douvris, Chris, Edward Bentil, Isaac Ayensu, Clement Osei Akoto, Isaac Kingsley Amponsah, Joseph Adu, and **Derek Bussan**. "Trace Metals in Cannabis Seized by Law Enforcement in Ghana and Multivariate Analysis to Distinguish among Different Cannabis Farms." *Toxics* 10, no. 10 (2022): 567.
2. **Burns, Rachel L., Raegan Alexander, Liliya Snaychuk**, John C. Edwards, Neil Fitzgerald, Pei Gao, Donghui Quan, Chris Douvris, Trey Vaughan, and **Derek D. Bussan**. "A fast, straightforward and inexpensive method for the authentication of Baijiu spirit samples by fluorescence spectroscopy." *Beverages* 7, no. 3 (2021): 65.
3. Douvris, Chris, Vaughan Trey, **Derek Bussan**, Georgios Bartzas, and Robert Thomas. "How ICP-OES changed the face of trace element analysis: Review of the global application landscape." *Science of The Total Environment* (2023): 167242.
4. **Bussan, Derek D., Liliya Snaychuk**, Georgios Bartzas, and Chris Douvris. "Quantification of trace elements in surgical and KN95 face masks widely used during the SARS-COVID-19 pandemic." *Science of The Total Environment* 814 (2022): 151924.
5. **Bussan, Derek D.,** Chris Douvris, and James V. Cizdziel. "Mercury methylation potentials in sediments of an ancient cypress wetland using species-specific isotope dilution GC-ICP-MS." *Molecules* 27, no. 15 (2022): 4911.
6. **Snaychuk, Liliya**, Trey Vaughan, **Zachary Ullery**, Chris Douvris, and **Derek D. Bussan**. "Inductively Coupled Plasma Optical Emission Spectroscopy (ICP-OES) Analysis of Trace Metals in Cigarette Litter collected at McNeese State University in Lake Charles, LA, United States." *Methods & Objects of Chemical Analysis/Metody & Obekty Himičeskogo Analiza* 17, no. 1 (2022).

7. Douvris, Chris, Christos Lampropoulos, David Matatov, Donald J. Wink, Aleksey E. Kuznetsov, and **Derek Bussan**. "Synthesis and structural characterization of the first stable cycloheptatrienyl metal complexes bearing a CF3 moiety. DFT investigations of structures, energetics, NBO charges, and frontier MOs of W-CF3 and Mo-CF3 with η7-C7H7 and η5-C5H5." *Polyhedron* 221 (2022): 115875.

8. Douvris, Chris, David Matatov, **Derek Bussan**, Christos Lampropoulos, and Donald J. Wink. "Synthesis, Characterization, and X-ray Crystallography, of the First Cyclohexadienyl Trifluoromethyl Metal Complex (η5-C6H7) Fe (CO) 2CF3." *Molecules* 27, no. 21 (2022): 7595.

9. **Bussan, Derek, Austin Harris**, and Chris Douvris. "Monitoring of selected trace elements in sediments of heavily industrialized areas in Calcasieu Parish, Louisiana, United States by inductively coupled plasma-optical emission spectroscopy (ICP-OES)." *Microchemical Journal* 144 (2019): 51-55.

10. Materer, Nicholas F., Allen Apblett, Evgueni B. Kadossov, **Derek Bussan**, Meagan Bobo, Grit Kupgan, and Dylan Dyer. "Experimental and Computation Studies of the Reaction of Hydrogen Peroxide and Methyl Hydroperoxide on Molybdenum Hydrogen Bronze Surfaces." *Topics in Catalysis* 61 (2018): 1183-1192.

11. **Bussan, Derek D.**, Clifford A. Ochs, Colin R. Jackson, Tarun Anumol, Shane A. Snyder, and James V. Cizdziel. "Concentrations of select dissolved trace elements and anthropogenic organic compounds in the Mississippi River and major tributaries during the summer of 2012 and 2013." *Environmental monitoring and assessment* 189 (2017): 1-18.

12. **Bussan, Derek D., Ryan F. Sessums**, and James V. Cizdziel. "Activated carbon and biochar reduce mercury methylation potentials in aquatic sediments." *Bulletin of environmental contamination and toxicology* 96 (2016): 536-539.

13. Plukienė, R., A. Plukis, A. Puzas, R. Gvozdaitė, V. Barkauskas, G. Duškesas, J. V. Cizdziel, **D. Bussan**, and V. Remeikis. "Actinides input to the dose in the irradiated graphite of RBMK-1500 reactor." *Nuclear Engineering and Design* 300 (2016): 530-535.

14. **Bussan, Derek D., Ryan F. Sessums**, and James V. Cizdziel. "Direct mercury analysis in environmental solids by ICP-MS with on-line sample ashing and mercury pre-concentration using a direct mercury analyzer." *Journal of Analytical Atomic Spectrometry* 30, no. 7 (2015): 1668-1672.

15. Reidy, Lorlyn, Rachel Williams, **Derek Bussan**, Steve Brewer, and James V. Cizdziel. "Elemental fingerprinting of gypsum drywall using sector field ICP-MS and multivariate statistics." *International Journal of Environmental Analytical Chemistry* 94, no. 13 (2014): 1273-1287.

MY TIME
Spending time with my family.
Officiating High School and College Baseball/Softball Games.
Increasing my external network via internal and external collaborations.
Reading inspiration books such as Winning by Jack Welch and Water Dog by Richard Wolters.
Visiting my family back home in Iowa.
Leveraging AI as a resource to optimize and elevate work performance.

REFERENCES:
First name Lastname, Ph.D.
Position title
Organization
City, State
Email_address@example.com
T: 111.222.3333

The preceding section showcased a comprehensive resume. In certain situations,

mainly industry or as a second resume source, employers might request a more concise

version, typically limited to two pages. To demonstrate how to effectively condense a

resume while maintaining its essential elements, I have included a shortened version of

the previously detailed resume below:"

Authors 1-2-page resume:

Derek D. Bussan PHONE: 111.222.3333 | E-MAIL: author@hopemydog.com 112233 1st Avenue North, Somewhere, IA 52001

EDUCATION
- MBA, Eastern Kentucky University, 2022
- Ph.D., Analytical Chemistry, University of Mississippi, 2015
- M.S., Inorganic Chemistry, Oklahoma State University, 2011
- B.A., General Chemistry, Minor in Mathematics, University of Iowa, 2004

PROFESSIONAL EXPERIENCE

Research Chemistry Manager, United States Department of Agriculture (2/23-Present)
- Oversaw Nutritional Analytic Laboratory operations; managed a budget of $X/year.
- Achieved cost reduction in instrument agreement from $K to $XK.
- Involved in budget preparation, equipment procurement, personnel management, and research oversight.
- Key roles in sample preparation, operating advanced laboratory instruments, and directing research studies.
- Authored and reviewed scientific papers and abstracts, contributing to nutritional analysis methodologies.
- Participated in scientific meetings and workshops for cutting-edge analytical methodologies.

Adjunct Marketing Instructor, University of North Dakota (August 2023-Present)
- Specialized in Business Communications and Negotiations.
- Employed interactive teaching methods for practical skill enhancement in professional communication.

Assistant Professor, Chemistry, Eastern Kentucky University (08/19-02/23)
- Increased program enrollment, resulting in significant revenue growth.
- Managed undergraduate research projects and academic collaborations.
- Served as a faculty senator and academic advisor.

Assistant Professor, Chemistry, McNeese State University (08/17-08/19)
- Secured a $718,000 Equipment Enhancement Grant.
- Led the Forensic Chemistry Unit and assisted in the acquisition of new laboratory instruments.

Senior Scientist/Post Doc, Lancaster Eurofins/Altria (2016 –2017)
- Managed trace metals lab; led a worldwide metals proficiency study.
- Developed methods for trace elements analysis in tobacco products.

Post-Doctoral Research Associate, Oak Ridge National Laboratory (2015 -2016)
- Developed analytical methods using HPLC-ICP-MS for element separation.

PROFESSIONAL MEMBERSHIPS
- American Chemical Society (2012-present)
- Editorial Board Member, Biological Trace Element Research (2023-present)
- Reviewer, Multidisciplinary Digital Publishing Institute (2021-present)

SELECTED PUBLICATIONS
- Authored and co-authored 15 peer-reviewed publications in esteemed journals.
- Corresponding author on a review paper in Science of The Total Environment (Impact Factor: 9.8).

PERSONAL INTERESTS
- Family time, officiating sports, reading, leveraging AI for work optimization.

REFERENCES Available upon request.

As illustrated, tailoring a resume's length can be quite straightforward. The key is to align it with the expectations of your prospective employer. Academic institutions often prefer more detailed resumes, whereas federal and state entities look for specific qualifications and competencies. This might necessitate submitting a comprehensive 'long' resume to meet HR criteria and a succinct 'short' version for the hiring committee's convenience. Should there be any need for further details, the hiring committee can always refer to the longer version for comprehensive information. For industry positions, a 2–3-page resume is generally ideal.

Remember, these insights stem from my personal experiences; your journey might dictate a different approach. Therefore, adapt your resume in a way that feels most authentic and effective for you.

The essence of a compelling resume includes your contact information at the top, followed by your educational background, placing the most recent or relevant degree first. Next, detail your work experience, highlighting key achievements and responsibilities. Consider bolding certain impactful keywords for emphasis, using my resume as a guiding example. Towards the end, include professional memberships, accolades, and publications.

I've always found it enriching to mention hobbies, pets, or leisure activities. Showing a well-rounded personality can be appealing to potential employers. And, of course, conclude with your references. Armed with these insights, you're well on your way to crafting a resume that stands out, paving the way for those interview calls. If you're not landing interviews, it might be a sign to reassess either the roles you're applying for or your resume. Conversely, if you're getting interviews but not job offers, it could be time to polish your interviewing skills. And that smoothly transitions us to our next vital topic: Applying for a Job!

CHAPTER 3: JOB APPLICATIONS

Where should I start? The process of applying for a job has advanced significantly. Gone are the days when one had to sift through newspaper and magazine ads. Nowadays, and potentially even more so 20-50 years from when I write this, the job application landscape could be completely different. Currently, and this has been the case for some time, the best way to find a job is through 'who you know'—in other words, your network. If you start asking around your professional network, chances are someone will know of an opportunity or position they want to fill. Whether this is the opportunity you're looking for is another question. However, if you are unemployed, beggars can't be choosers. Yet, you still need to know your worth, even if it's your first job.

In my opinion and best judgement, the best place to find your first or next opportunity is through:

Who you know/your network!

It's interesting that I believe the best place to start is by who you know. While this hasn't changed, what has evolved are the online avenues for finding employment. After tapping into your network, one of the first places I recommend is indeed.com. As a disclaimer, none of these job boards have paid me for endorsements; I wish they had, but that's not been my luck. I'm just trying to be honest while giving you, the job applicant, the best avenues out there. What I like about Indeed is that you can type in a job title and location to generate a search query. If you're still in college or high school, try typing in a job you're interested in and see how many listings you get. For instance, a search for 'nursing' in December 2023 yielded over 600,000 jobs, whereas 'paleontologist' only brought up a dozen or so opportunities. Keep in mind that these numbers can change, but the market ratios are likely to remain similar.

Next, I highly recommend LinkedIn. It's a social networking site aimed at professional networking and job searching. There's a 'Jobs' tab where you can enter your desired job and location. For example, a search for 'nursing' on LinkedIn on the same day I searched on indeed revealed close to 1 million job results, indicating that nursing is a viable career path. The reason for the discrepancy is that I have found that LinkedIn will sometimes list the same job twice. What sets LinkedIn apart is its ability to sort jobs by various filters and to show connections in your network related to a job search.

For those looking for a job in academia, HigherEdJobs is an excellent resource. It's not just for professor roles; you can find a variety of positions within the academic setting. For example, information technology, curriculum design, admissions, administrative assistants, alumni relations, athletics, food services, facilities management, legal, police

and public safety, sales, marketing, communications and so many more opportunities.

For federal or state jobs, www.usajobs.gov is the go-to for federal opportunities, and

governmentjobs.com for state, county, and city jobs. These websites have similar

search features but are tailored to their respective sectors. For example, on USAJOBS,

you can search by job series, such as the 0500 series for accounting and finance roles.

As of the time this book was written there are currently 343 job series within the

general schedule (GS) payscale. Please keep in mind that there are some federal

agencies that do not use USAJOBS, however you will find most civilian opportunities

on USAJOBS.

If you're still in college, consider searching for 'Pathways' on USAJOBS. This program

is designed to provide students with a pathway into federal employment. We'll discuss

later in this book what makes a good company or organization to work for. You'll find

that government jobs, at all levels, often offer attractive benefits. However, if you're

considering a state, county, or city job, keep in mind that your benefits and service time

might not transfer as easily as within the federal system. Another benefit of working for

the public sector is that there is often pay transparency. What do I mean by that is that you can find pay charts for a specific labor grade, or if that is not available type in an internet search browser the organization and job title that you are interested in and usually that is a good way to find out the typical pay, even better if you know someone with the same exact title that you would be coming in at. What you are going to find out is that this information will be important when it comes to the negotiating table.

Some of the things you want to look for are how much the job pays, and whether you can find a job in the area where you want to live. Consider what types of opportunities there are for growth. If you graduate with 50 students from your institution in your chosen major and there are only 300 jobs nationwide, you should think twice about that major, as there may be limited opportunities. I am not trying to discourage you from doing what you love, but there must be a practical aspect to the job search as well!

In conclusion, the opportunity you choose depends on whether it's the right fit for you, but also consider future opportunities and benefits. Some state and city jobs may even offer better health and retirement benefits than many industrial and federal opportunities.

This leads us to our next topic of interviewing techniques.

CHAPTER 4 INTERVIEWING TECHNIQUES

Now that your resume has been reviewed by either an HR specialist or the hiring manager/committee, the next crucial step is preparing for the interview. It's not uncommon for the first interview to be conducted by an HR generalist rather than the hiring manager. This initial screening ensures that a) the candidate is still interested in the position, b) the candidate's actual qualifications correspond to what's presented on paper, and c) the candidate's compensation expectations align with the role's budget. If you present yourself as a genuinely nice person and have a realistic grasp of the expected salary, you're likely to progress to the hiring manager's interview.

The initial interview is often held over the phone or, increasingly, via online platforms such as Zoom or Teams. To maintain fairness, all candidates are typically asked the same set of questions. This consistency is crucial for the hiring manager/committee to make direct comparisons between candidates.

Even if the interview is conducted over the phone or through an online platform, I recommend dressing up. Your appearance does matter, as it conveys professionalism. Good lighting is also essential for video interviews. I recall being part of an interview committee where a candidate was in a poorly lit room when they interviewed via

Zoom. The lack of visibility created an uncomfortable atmosphere and unfortunately didn't work in the candidate's favor. This situation demonstrates the importance of presenting yourself well. How you conduct yourself in an interview can reflect how you might interact with potential customers, clients, stakeholders, or students in a professional setting.

Furthermore, ensure you have a reliable internet connection and a quiet environment for the interview. I once found myself renting a room at a library for an online interview, which proved to be a wise decision. The excellent internet connection, absence of noise disturbances, and good lighting helped me advance to the next interview stage, which was the on-site interview.

Note that not all interview questions will be technical. Many will probe how you function in a team environment, a crucial aspect of most modern workplaces. For managerial or supervisory roles, expect queries about your ability to motivate team members, as leadership is as much about inspiration as it is about technical knowledge.

Sample Interview Questions:

1. Can you describe a challenging project you worked on and how you managed it?
2. How do you handle stress and pressure in a work environment?

3. Describe a situation where you had to work closely with a difficult coworker. How did you handle it?

4. Can you give an example of how you have motivated others in a work setting?

5. Tell me about a time when you had to adapt to significant changes at work.

6. How do you prioritize your tasks in a fast-paced work environment?

7. Describe your experience with managing a team. What approach do you take?

8. Can you discuss a time when you had to make an unpopular decision? How did you handle the fallout?

9. How do you assess the success of a project? Give an example.

10. What strategies do you use to stay current with industry trends and developments?

By effectively addressing these questions, you can showcase your problem-solving, communication, and leadership skills, which are invaluable in any professional role.

Many interviews today employ the ***"STAR"*** technique, a method designed to elicit detailed and structured responses from candidates. STAR stands for Situation, Task, Action, and Result. This technique helps interviewers understand not just what you did, but how you did it and the outcomes of your actions. It encourages you to present your experiences in a narrative format that is both comprehensive and easy to follow.

When responding to questions using the STAR technique, you should begin by describing the Situation – setting the scene and providing the necessary context. Next, outline the Task – what your responsibility or challenge was in that situation. Then, describe the Action – the specific steps you took to address the task. Finally, conclude with the Result – the outcome of your actions, ideally highlighting any positive impact or lessons learned.

The STAR technique is particularly effective in interviews as it allows candidates to showcase their problem-solving skills, decision-making processes, and ability to adapt to new challenges. By structuring your answers in this way, you provide the interviewer with clear, concise, and relevant examples that demonstrate your capabilities.

Sample Questions Using the STAR Technique:

1. **Describe a time when you had to resolve a conflict within a team.**

   - **Situation:** In my previous role as a project manager, our team faced a significant conflict when two key team members disagreed on the direction of a project.

   - **Task:** As the project manager, it was my responsibility to mediate the conflict and keep the project on track.

- **Action:** I organized a meeting for a candid discussion, allowing each team member to voice their concerns and proposed a compromise.

- **Result:** The conflict was resolved, the project was completed successfully, and the team's communication improved.

2. **Tell me about a challenging project you managed and how you ensured its success.**

- **Situation:** I was assigned a project that was behind schedule and over budget at my last job.

- **Task:** My goal was to bring the project back on track without compromising on quality.

- **Action:** I restructured the team's workflow and implemented progress meetings.

- **Result:** We met the deadline within budget, and my team was recognized for our efficiency.

3. **Recall a time when you had to adapt to a significant change at work.**

- **Situation:** Following a company merger, our processes and team structures underwent significant changes.

- **Task:** As a team leader, I had to ensure a smooth transition for my team.

- **Action:** I participated in integration training and communicated changes effectively to my team.

- **Result:** The team adapted well to the changes, improving our productivity and receiving positive feedback from management.

By using the STAR technique in your interview responses, you can demonstrate your skills and experiences in a structured, engaging, and effective way. This approach not only helps you to stay focused and relevant but also enables the interviewer to clearly understand and evaluate your suitability for the role.

Preparing for the Onsite Interview

Congratulations on advancing to the onsite interview stage, often the final step in the interview process. Your preparation for this crucial phase starts with extensive research into the organization. Prior to even the phone or online interview, it's imperative to have a deep understanding of the company's history, products, culture, and recent developments. Showcasing this knowledge during the interview not only impresses the interviewers but also demonstrates your keen interest in becoming part of their team. Remember, knowing the exact nature of the company's business is fundamental. You don't want to talk about bicycle manufacturing techniques when the company is known for making cars.

Presentation is just as important in the onsite interview. Consider investing in professional attire if you haven't already done so. Making a good first impression is crucial, and dressing appropriately can significantly contribute to this.

Familiarize yourself with the town or city where the interview is located. Using tools like Google Maps to scout the area, including your hotel and the route to the interview location, is a practical step. This sort of preparation not only helps with punctuality but also shows your commitment and attention to detail.

Make sure you are well-rested and have a good meal before the interview. It's natural to feel a mix of excitement and nervousness, but maintaining your regular routine as much as possible can help. On the day of the interview, aim to arrive early, even if it means waiting in your car or in a reception area.

The onsite interview can range from a straightforward process to a comprehensive security check, depending on the company and its policies. You will likely meet the hiring manager initially and possibly an HR liaison who will discuss employee benefits. Being genuine and authentic is key here.

Onsite interviews can vary in length and format as I have found out through my own personal experiences. I have experienced everything from a quick, one-hour interview to a full two-day process worth of interviewing, which included delivering a 50-minute presentation. If you have a time slot for a presentation, be sure that you practice ensuring you stay within the allotted timeframe, you don't want to be the interviewee whose presentation was only 15 minutes for a 50-minute presentation, or to run over 15 minutes of the allotted presentation time. This could also show a lack of respect for the people that are interviewing you as they often have other obligations during the day of your interview.

During your visit, you may also meet with senior executives. Every interaction, including meals with potential colleagues or superiors, is part of the interview. Here's where the fun part comes in – remember to be sensible with your food choices. You're not a competitive eater trying to dethrone Joey Chestnut or Miku Sudo in Nathan's Famous Hot Dog Eating Contest. Select something moderate from the menu. It's a chance to display good judgment and social skills.

Throughout the interview process, stay positive, enthusiastic, and demonstrate your willingness to contribute. This approach should be a part of your current professional or academic life, and it's particularly important here.

After the interview, send a follow-up email within 24 hours. This shows appreciation for the time interviewers took out of their busy schedules to meet with you.

This section hopefully provided you with a comprehensive understanding of the onsite interview process, emphasizing the importance of company research, presentation, and etiquette. Armed with these insights, you're now ready to excel in your interviews. Go out there and make a great impression!

CHAPTER 5 IDENTIFYING QUALITY EMPLOYERS

Navigating the modern job market requires a keen understanding of what makes an employer stand out. It's not solely about the allure of a high salary; the hallmarks of a quality employer encompass a broad range of benefits, including retirement plans, comprehensive medical coverage, generous time off policies, and a commitment to work-life balance. This complex tapestry of factors collectively defines an employer's value.

Extensive Research for Finding Exceptional Employers: To identify these standout employers, deep and thorough research is indispensable. Utilize a variety of platforms like Indeed, Glassdoor, Reddit, and LinkedIn to gather insights into different company cultures. These platforms provide a wealth of information, from employee reviews to salary data. Moreover, tapping into your professional networks can offer candid, behind-the-scenes views of potential employers, providing a clearer picture of their operations and culture.

1. Retirement Plans and Financial Security: Investigating an employer's approach to retirement planning is key. While 401(k) plans are common, the gold standard remains the pension plan or defined benefit plan. These plans offer a sense of financial security in retirement, providing a stable income stream

independent of stock market fluctuations. The onus of managing the fund lies with the employer, offering peace of mind to employees. Understanding the nuances of different retirement plans is crucial in assessing an employer's quality.

2. In-Depth Healthcare Benefits Analysis: Dive deep into the healthcare benefits offered. This includes comparing premiums, deductibles, and the extent of coverage. It's important to consider the range of options provided, from Health Savings Accounts (HSAs) to more traditional options like PPOs and HMOs, and how these plans fit with your healthcare needs.

3. 401(k) Plans and Employer Contributions: Look closely at the specifics of 401(k) plans, particularly the employer match rate and the variety of investment choices available. These details can significantly affect your long-term financial health and retirement readiness.

4. Career Progression and Professional Development: Evaluate the company's commitment to employee growth. This includes opportunities for training, mentorship, and clear pathways for advancement. A company that invests in its employees' development is indicative of a long-term commitment to their workforce.

5. Vacation and PTO Policies: A company's stance on vacation and paid time off is a direct reflection of its work culture. Generous time-off policies indicate a recognition of the importance of work-life balance and employee well-being.

6. Understanding Salary Structures: Getting a clear picture of potential earnings and the trajectory for salary growth is crucial. In the private sector, where pay scales might be less transparent, this becomes even more important.

7. Flexibility with Remote Work and Work Hours: With the evolving dynamics of the modern workplace, the availability of remote work options and flexible working hours is increasingly important. These options can greatly influence work-life balance and overall job satisfaction.

8. Evaluating Company Culture and Values: A positive and engaging company culture, which values diversity, inclusivity, and environmental responsibility, is a significant indicator of a quality employer. Understanding a company's core values and how they align with your own is key.

9. Employee Feedback and Reviews: Regularly reviewing employee feedback can

provide invaluable insights into the company's management style, culture, and operational ethos. Look for recurring themes in reviews to get a sense of the overall employee experience.

10. Additional Benefits and Perks: Additional benefits, such as tuition reimbursement, wellness programs, mental health support, and childcare facilities, can greatly enhance the overall employment experience. These benefits show an employer's commitment to the holistic well-being of their employees.

11. Assessing Financial Stability and Growth Potential: Researching the company's financial health and its plans for future growth is essential for gauging job security and career advancement opportunities. A stable and growing company can offer a more secure career path.

12. Work Environment and Employee Engagement Initiatives: The physical work environment and the company's efforts to create a positive, engaging, and supportive workplace are important factors. Consider how the company fosters a sense of community and engagement among its employees.

In summary, identifying a quality employer requires a comprehensive evaluation of a myriad of factors, from tangible benefits such as salary and healthcare, to more intangible aspects like company culture, career development opportunities, and work environment. The goal is to find an employer that meets your immediate needs and aligns with your long-term aspirations and personal values. Through meticulous research and self-reflection, you can make an informed decision about your next career move. Special attention to retirement planning, particularly the availability of a pension plan, can be a key differentiator in today's job market, offering a level of financial security and stability that is highly valued.

CHAPTER 6: ESSENTIAL SKILLS BEYOND THE SCHOOL CURRICULUM

Where do I start with this section? In all honesty, entire encyclopedia sets could be written on this subject. One consideration that I believe everyone should ponder when picking a career is the ***return on investment***. For example, you may be an exceptional xylophone player, but will that skill equate to being able to support you and your family? It's the same with picking and choosing the right career; some start off in the $30k range, while others may begin well above $100k. Therefore, deciding on a career path that can provide a suitable income for you and your family needs careful consideration.

Retirement/Social security:

When I was in undergraduate or even within my graduate studies, no one taught me anything about retirement. I understand that relying solely on social security may not provide enough income for some people to live on, but it is a start. Please understand that I am not a financial advisor, so do seek advice from a qualified financial advisor. However, if you visit the social security website, www.ssa.gov, you can conduct a search. Eventually, you will come across a section that states the following:

"You must earn at least 40 Social Security credits to qualify for Social Security benefits. You earn credits when you work and pay Social Security taxes. The number of credits does not affect the amount of benefits you receive. We use the number of credits you've earned to determine your eligibility for retirement or disability benefits, Medicare, and your family's eligibility for survivors benefits when you die. We cannot pay benefits to you if you don't have enough credits."

This means if you work a job and do not see social security being deducted from your paycheck, you may not be contributing to social security benefits. Each year, the amount required to earn one credit changes; as of 2023, the maximum number of credits you can earn per year is four. In 2023, you need $1,640 in covered earnings for each credit, and for the maximum of four credits, you must earn $6,560. Essentially, it would take a minimum of 10 years for you to earn sufficient social security benefits. For information on disability and other benefits such as survivor benefits, please visit the social security website. I have always believed that retirement should be approached as a three-legged stool, with one of those legs being social security. When to collect social security is up to you; in my age bracket, I can start collecting when I turn 62 and receive my maximum benefit at 70. Waiting until 70 could mean a difference of thousands of dollars, but it's important to remember that people don't live forever.

When considering when to start receiving your social security benefits, the social security website provides actuarial life tables. If you visit www.ssa.gov and search for 'actuarial life table', you will find various life tables over the years. For instance, considering the Period Life Table from 2020, as referenced in the 2023 Trustees Report, and contemplating the possibility of claiming my maximum social security benefits at age 70, I find that only 68,565 of the original 100,000 males born in my cohort are still alive. At that age, there is a 13.59% chance of dying within the year. For females, this number increases to 80,537 out of the initial 100,000 remain, with a 15.82 percent chance of dying. Generally, females tend to live longer than males in the United States. The decision to start collecting social security is personal and should be made with your financial advisor and family. However, I plan to start taking mine out before the age of 65 to enjoy some of the benefits before I pass away.

Pension plan aka defined benefit plan:

The second leg of retirement planning if your employee offers this benefit would be your pension plan. As I mentioned earlier, a pension plan is like a never-ending pot of money, typically having a vesting period. This period is the amount of time you need to work for an employer before you are vested in the program. A common vesting period is five years, meaning you must work for that employer for five years to be vested in their pension plan. Many public entities use the following formula: number of years worked, multiplied by a certain multiplier, times your highest average salary over three years of service. For example, if I worked for an employer for 10 years, with a multiplier of 1.00 and my highest average three-year salary was $100k, I would be able to collect $833.33 per month for the rest of my life. The starting age for collecting pension and any associated penalties are defined by the employer. If you are so lucky to work for an employer that has restricted stock units, there usually is a vesting period for this benefit as well, however this topic is beyond the scope of this book.

401k aka defined contribution plan:

The third leg of your retirement benefits, in my opinion, will be your 401k. As of 2023, the maximum contribution is $22.5K, and in 2024, this amount is set to increase to $23K. Please note that when you reach a certain age, generally 50 and older, you can make so-called catch-up contributions. This is designed to help earners who didn't have the resources to contribute when they were younger. The annual catch-up contribution in 2023 was $7,500. Most of the time, you can choose to make your 401k contributions either pre-tax or post-tax. The advantage of pre-tax contributions is that it lowers your taxable income. For instance, if I made $100K in 2023 and contributed $22.5K pre-tax, my taxable income would reduce to $77.5K. On the other hand, with post-tax contributions, you pay taxes on the contributions now but don't have to pay federal taxes on them later. Keep in mind that states and cities may have their own tax codes, so seek advice from a certified tax professional when deciding whether to contribute pre-tax or post-tax. In the post-tax scenario, if I contributed $22.5K, my taxable income would remain $100K.

Regarding the 401k, you should expect slow and steady growth, in contrast to volatile meme or high-risk options. It's advisable to ideally stay with the so-called blue-chip stock options. Investing in the S&P 500 early in your career and consistently contributing can lead to significant growth. Historically since 1980, the S&P 500 has had an averaged annual return on investment between 11 and 12%. However, remember that the S&P 500 is based on the stock market, which can have periods of decline. During these periods of decline, the value of your 401k may decrease, but it also presents an opportunity to invest in shares at a lower cost. As you get closer to retirement, it's generally advisable to consult with a retirement professional. You may want to shift to less risky investments, such as a secured money market type portfolio, offering lower growth but less risk. This strategy can be crucial, as you will likely need this money for retirement and might not want to wait several years for your investments to recover.

With social security, a pension plan, and a healthy 401k, you should be well on your way to an enjoyable retirement.

Another strategy for enhancing financial growth is by ***investing in land***, which serves as a strategic and valuable financial asset.

Investing in land within the real estate sector presents a distinctive and advantageous opportunity compared to owning buildings or other property types. One of the most compelling aspects of land ownership is its potential as a long-term financial asset, particularly considering the finite nature of land availability. As they are not making any more land, the value of existing land can appreciate significantly over time. This factor, combined with relatively lower maintenance and tax burdens, makes land a strategic investment. Here are some crucial points to consider about the financial benefits of owning land:

1. **Finite Resource**: Land is a limited resource, which inherently adds to its value. As the available land does not increase, but demand often does,

especially in growing areas, this scarcity can drive up the value of your investment.

2. **Lower Maintenance Requirements**: Raw land typically requires less upkeep compared to properties with structures. Without buildings to repair or tenants to manage, the reduced need for maintenance translates to lower costs and less personal involvement.

3. **Reduced Tax Liabilities**: The property taxes on undeveloped land are often lower than those on developed real estate. This is because the assessed value of raw land is usually less than that of developed property, leading to a more cost-effective investment in the long run.

4. **Appreciation Potential**: In growing or developing areas, the value of land tends to increase. This appreciation potential is heightened by the fact that land is a finite resource, making it more valuable as available spaces in urban areas diminish.

5. **Flexibility in Use**: As a landowner, you have the option to develop, hold, or sell the land depending on market conditions and personal financial goals. This flexibility allows for strategic planning and potential significant returns.

6. **Lower Initial Investment**: Typically, acquiring undeveloped land requires a smaller initial investment compared to purchasing developed property, making it more accessible for those entering the real estate market.

7. **Simplicity in Acquisition**: The process of buying land is generally less complex, with fewer factors like building inspections and tenant issues to consider.

8. **Diversification in Investment Portfolio**: Including land in your portfolio diversifies your investments, providing a buffer against market volatility in real estate.

9. **Potential for Passive Income**: Though often seen as a long-term asset, land can generate passive income through avenues like agricultural leasing or billboard advertising.

In conclusion, land ownership, as a finite and appreciating asset, offers a unique mix of benefits, including lower maintenance and tax burdens, along with the potential for significant value appreciation and flexible usage. It's an attractive option for those seeking to diversify their investment portfolio in real estate, sans the complexities and costs associated with buildings. However, it's essential to thoroughly research and evaluate factors like location, market trends, and development prospects before investing in land.

Another aspect often not discussed in a typical academic setting is that your first job after graduation may not be your last. Therefore, if you don't get the salary and benefits you want from your first job, use it to gain invaluable experience for your resume. This experience will make you more competitive for your dream organization in the future.

Communication, writing, and negotiating skills require practice, meaning you need to step out of your comfort zone and start developing these skills. You won't spontaneously develop the gift of gab if you never engage in conversation. Similarly, if you don't practice writing, how will you be able to quickly generate a report for your boss? Accepting the first price offered in a negotiation can cost you significantly, not just in terms of salary, but also when negotiating for a house, a vehicle, or other important purchases. Skilled negotiators can save a lot of money for an organization, which can be a valuable asset to you, as not everyone possesses this skill. For practice, the next time you need a vehicle, try seeing how low you can get the car salesperson to go. Let them ponder your offer, then return and negotiate even lower, perhaps by conducting market research on a similar car in a different location. If you're willing to travel, you might find deals tens of thousands of dollars lower than at your local dealership. Check if they can match that deal or come close. This skill can similarly be applied to salary negotiations, vacation time, bonuses, etc. Remember, at certain pay grades, there might only be so much that HR and your hiring manager can do, so let that be up to them.

The ***cost of living*** varies greatly depending on your location. For example, earning $100K in Grand Forks, ND, goes much further than it would in NYC. Renting an apartment in NYC might cost $5,000 per month, whereas in Grand Forks, it might only be $1,500 per month. That $3,500 monthly difference could be invested in a savings account, retirement account, or other forms of investment, rather than just covering higher living costs. I often look at housing on zillow.com or bestplaces.net/cost-of-living for cost-of-living comparisons. For instance, to maintain a standard of living of $100K in Grand Forks in 2023, you would need $196,503 in NYC, with one of the major differences being the median home cost – around $240K in Grand Forks compared to approximately $677K in NYC.

One area that I believe schools often fail to emphasize is the importance of ***eating healthily and maintaining a good exercise routine***. The food you consume is critical as it fuels your body with all the necessary nutrients. If your job entails a lot of manual or mental labor, what you eat significantly impacts your performance. Additionally, if your occupation doesn't involve much physical exercise, it's important to dedicate some time to this activity. Regular exercise, when done correctly, is beneficial for health and can increase work productivity by fostering a better mindset. Exercise also contributes to overall well-being.

Setting aside time for family and friends is crucial. As the life tables from the social security website reminds us, our time on earth is finite, so it's important to cherish moments with those we love and care for. I've noticed that when switching jobs, I generally lose contact with most of my former colleagues. This isn't due to any disagreements; it's simply because they are not as closely bonded as family and friends. However, whenever I've switched jobs, I've always maintained contact with my family and close friends. Finding a colleague who becomes a good friend can be incredibly rewarding. I keep in touch with former colleagues who are now my best friends. We consult each other for advice, share ideas, and experience life events together. Spending a lot of time at work inevitably leads to forming bonds, and ideally, these bonds should be positive experiences.

Home ownership:

Owning a home and relocating for a job both involve substantial expenses. Below, I outline several reasons explaining why these activities can be financially demanding:

1. **Initial Costs of Home Ownership**: The journey of home ownership begins with significant upfront costs. This includes the down payment, which is often the most substantial expense, typically ranging from 3.5% to 20% of the home's purchase price. Additionally, there are closing costs, which can include loan origination fees, appraisal fees, title searches, title insurance, surveys, taxes, and

credit report charges. These costs often amount to 2% to 5% of the purchase price of the home.

2. **Ongoing Expenses**: Beyond the initial investment, homeowners face a variety of recurring expenses. This includes mortgage payments, property taxes, homeowners insurance, and potentially, private mortgage insurance (PMI) if the down payment was less than 20%. Maintenance and repair costs are also a significant part of the ongoing expenses, which can vary widely but often average around 1% of the home's value annually. Utilities and homeowners association (HOA) fees can also add to the monthly financial burden.

3. **The Cost of Moving for a Job**: Relocating for a job involves a variety of expenses. If you own a home and decide to move, you might face the costs of selling your home, which include real estate agent fees, staging and home improvements to make the property more appealing, and possibly capital gains tax if the home has significantly appreciated in value.

4. **Relocation Expenses**: Direct relocation expenses include hiring movers, which can range from a few hundred to several thousand dollars depending on the distance and the amount of belongings. There are also travel expenses, temporary lodging if the new home is not immediately available, and potential storage fees for belongings. Additionally, if moving to a location with a higher cost of living, this can represent a long-term increase in daily living expenses.

5. **Indirect Costs and Considerations**: Moving for a job also comes with indirect costs, such as the emotional toll of leaving behind a community and familiar surroundings. There may be costs associated with establishing yourself in a new community, such as joining clubs or activities to meet new people. If moving to a different state or country, there might be legal and administrative costs involved in establishing residency, obtaining necessary documents, or even dealing with different tax laws.

6. **Long-Term Financial Implications**: The long-term financial impact of both home ownership and relocating for a job can be significant. Home ownership can be an investment, with the potential for the property value to increase over time. However, it also ties up a large amount of capital and can be less flexible than renting. On the other hand, relocating for a job might offer career advancement and potentially higher earnings, but it also involves the risk of the new position not being as stable or lucrative as anticipated.

7. **Preparation and Planning**: Effective planning and budgeting are essential to manage the costs associated with home ownership and job relocation. This might involve saving an emergency fund to cover unexpected home repairs or relocation costs, researching thoroughly before making any moves, and considering all financial implications of such significant life decisions.

Maintaining a **_financial safety net_** of 6-12 months' worth of savings is crucial, as it prepares you for unforeseen expenses that may arise.

1. **Job Security Uncertainty**: In today's volatile job market, layoffs, furloughs, and unexpected terminations are not uncommon. Having a savings cushion equivalent to 6-12 months of your regular expenses can provide the much-needed financial security during such periods. It allows you to continue meeting your essential needs, like housing, utilities, food, and healthcare, without the immediate pressure to find a new job.

2. **Health Emergencies**: Medical emergencies can arise without warning, and even with insurance, the costs can be significant. A robust savings account can help cover high deductibles, out-of-pocket expenses, and any loss of income during recovery.

3. **Natural Disasters and Home Repairs**: Homeowners and renters alike can face sudden, unexpected costs due to natural disasters like floods, earthquakes, or even smaller-scale incidents like a burst pipe. These events often come with expenses that aren't fully covered by insurance. A solid savings reserve can help manage these costs without resorting to high-interest loans.

4. **Career Transition Flexibility**: If you decide to change careers or need time to find a job that is a better fit, having a financial cushion allows you the flexibility to explore options without the urgency of immediate income.

5. **Mental Peace and Reduced Stress**: Financial instability is a significant source of stress. Knowing you have a financial safety net can provide mental peace, allowing you to focus on your immediate needs and long-term goals without the constant worry of financial ruin due to unforeseen circumstances.

6. **Avoiding Debt**: Without adequate savings, emergencies often lead to reliance on credit cards or loans, leading to a cycle of debt. A savings buffer can help you avoid this, preserving your credit score and saving you from high interest rates.

7. **Planning for the Future**: This savings buffer isn't just about emergencies; it's also a foundation for future financial plans, whether that's investing, purchasing property, or retirement savings.

To achieve this savings goal, consider setting up automatic transfers to a dedicated emergency fund, cutting down on non-essential expenses, and regularly reviewing and adjusting your savings plan. Remember, building this fund is a gradual process, and even small contributions can add up over time.

Maximizing Financial Potential Through *__Career Mobility__*

In today's dynamic job market, one of the most effective strategies for financial advancement is changing jobs. This approach can often lead to significant increases in income and benefits, paving the way for improved financial stability and growth. Here are some key points to consider about the financial benefits of job switching:

1. **Higher Salary Offers**: Changing jobs often comes with the opportunity for a higher salary. Employers typically offer competitive packages to attract skilled candidates, which can result in a substantial pay increase compared to incremental raises given by current employers.

2. **Negotiation Leverage**: When moving to a new job, there's an opportunity to negotiate not just for higher pay, but also for better benefits, bonuses, and other compensations. This leverage is often stronger when coming from a position of current employment, as opposed to negotiating raises internally.

3. **Career Advancement**: Job changes can lead to more significant career advancement opportunities. Moving to a new company might offer a higher position, more responsibilities, or a role that better aligns with long-term career goals, which in turn can lead to higher income.

4. **Expanded Skill Set and Experience**: Changing jobs often means learning new skills, adapting to different environments, and expanding professional networks. This can enhance your value in the job market, leading to higher earning potential in future roles.

5. **Avoiding Salary Complacency**: Staying in one job for an extended period can sometimes lead to salary complacency, where annual raises are minimal and don't keep pace with the market rate for your skills and experience. Job hopping at strategic intervals can ensure your salary stays competitive.

6. **Access to New Industries and Markets**: Changing jobs might also mean venturing into new industries or markets that have higher earning potentials or are experiencing growth, which can lead to more lucrative opportunities.

7. **Improved Job Satisfaction and Performance**: Often, a job change can lead to improved job satisfaction due to a better company culture, more aligned values, or a more desirable role. This increased satisfaction can enhance performance, leading to further financial rewards like bonuses and promotions.

8. **Risk vs. Reward Consideration**: While changing jobs can be financially beneficial, it's also essential to weigh the risks, such as job security, company stability, and the cultural fit of the new workplace.

In conclusion, changing jobs is a significant move with the potential to greatly enhance one's financial situation. However, it's crucial to approach this step thoughtfully, considering all the potential benefits and risks involved.

I've discovered the importance of having *hobbies and interests* outside of work as a means to connect with a diverse range of people. For example, my involvement in officiating sports like baseball, softball, and volleyball introduced me to individuals who were quite different from my colleagues at my regular 8-5 job. These people come from varied backgrounds, and it's a great opportunity to engage with others in the community. You never know what new opportunities might arise from these connections. Even if it doesn't directly benefit your career, it's rewarding to contribute positively to your community.

Additionally, some hobbies offer financial compensation, adding an extra perk. I often opted for hobbies that provided some income, and I used this additional money for personal or family enrichment. This extra income can also act as a financial buffer in case of an unexpected job loss.

Take your ***earned time off***. If you are on a probationary period, please use caution during this time, as sometimes you can be let go for no apparent reason. However, once you've earned that time off, use it to recharge. A recharged employee is more productive, as you will be refreshed and full of ideas.

Take advantage of ***networking opportunities***, whether that's going to a conference or a vendor's fair. There's always something to learn when meeting new people.

Embrace the culture of the place you've moved to. If you're like me and have moved from one end of the country to another, you won't magically change the people around you. I've learned to embrace their culture and bring positive experiences from my past to these new places. Also, be prepared for different weather, as I've lived in very hot and humid places, as well as very cold ones. Each place is unique, offering different activities and unique food and drink experiences.

Just **_be positive_**, have a positive outlook on life and your career, and usually, good things happen. If you believe it can happen, sometimes, just like in the movie 'Field of Dreams' where Kevin Costner keeps hearing **_'if you build it, they will come,'_** it can often work in life as well. Build upon yourself with experiences and knowledge, and good things will come to you!

CHAPTER 7 STUDENT/INSTRUCTOR EXERCISES

Introduction: As this book is intended for both students and instructors, I want to introduce various activities that are practical and applicable to the real world. While the primary readership might be students, these exercises are valuable regardless of whether they are assigned by your instructor. They provide hands-on experience in applying the concepts taught in this book.

Exercise for Chapter 2: Resume Building and Refinement

Objective: This exercise aims to enhance your resume, transforming it into an effective tool for job applications. You will begin with your current resume, analyze it critically, and make the necessary improvements.

Assignment Tasks:

1. Review Your Current Resume: Begin by examining your existing resume. This will be the starting point for your refinements.

2. Research Ideal Resume Formats: Investigate the most effective resume formats. Refer to the example provided in Chapter 1 for guidance. Understand the various sections, their proper sequencing, and their content requirements.

3. Identify Weaknesses: Pinpoint areas in your current resume that need improvement, such as formatting, content, and the use of action verbs and keywords.

4. Content Enhancement: Evaluate the content of your resume. Ensure that your experiences and skills are communicated effectively. Focus on highlighting your achievements, responsibilities, and quantifiable outcomes.

5. Formatting and Layout: Review the layout, font choice, and overall formatting. Aim for visual appeal and ease of skimming, maintaining consistent formatting throughout.

6. Tailoring for Specific Jobs: Tailor your resume to align with the job you are targeting. Incorporate relevant keywords and skills pertinent to that role.

7. Education and Additional Sections: Reassess your education section for completeness and organization. Consider adding sections like "Skills," "Certifications," "Awards," or "Volunteer Experience" where applicable.

8. Use of Action Verbs: Begin each bullet point under work experience with an action verb to add dynamism to your resume.

9. Proofreading: Thoroughly proofread your resume to eliminate spelling, grammatical, or typographical errors.

10. Peer Review: If possible, have your resume reviewed by a classmate or friend for additional feedback.

Submission Requirements:

1. Create an improved version of your resume, incorporating the elements discussed above.

2. Save your revised resume in a standard format (PDF or Word document) with a clear file name.

3. Submit your resume via the designated platform by the specified deadline.

Grading Criteria: Your resume will be evaluated based on clarity, organization, formatting, the relevance and customization of information, effective use of action verbs and keywords, and grammatical correctness. The improvement from your initial draft will also be considered.

Note: Retain a copy of your revised resume for future job applications. Remember, while this exercise may be for academic credit, the ultimate judge of your resume's effectiveness will be potential employers. Thus, it is in your best interest to put forth your best effort.

Exercise for Chapter 3: Mock Job Application Exercise for Chapter 2: "Navigating Modern Job Applications"

Background: This exercise is designed to simulate the modern job application process, emphasizing the importance of networking, online job boards, and understanding different sectors. It will help students develop practical skills in job searching and applying, including how to tailor applications to different types of jobs.

Scenario: Students are tasked with applying for a hypothetical job. They must choose a sector (private, academic, or government) and a specific job within that sector. The exercise involves researching the job, tailoring their application, and preparing a cover letter and resume suitable for the chosen position.

Instructions for Instructors:

1. Divide students into small groups and assign each group a different sector: private, academic, or government.

2. Instruct each group to select a specific job within their assigned sector. For instance, a marketing position in the private sector, an administrative assistant role in academia, or a finance officer in government.

3. Guide the groups to research their chosen job using relevant online platforms (such as Indeed, LinkedIn, HigherEdJobs, or USAJOBS).

4. Each student should create a tailored resume and cover letter for their selected job, using the information gathered from their research.

5. Encourage students to apply the principles of networking by identifying potential connections on platforms like LinkedIn that could help them in the application process.

Sample Job Application Tasks:

1. **Research and Selection:** Choose a job and conduct detailed research on the role and organization.

2. **Resume Creation:** Develop a resume tailored to the job, highlighting relevant skills and experiences.

3. **Cover Letter Writing:** Write a cover letter that addresses the specific requirements of the job and demonstrates knowledge about the organization.

4. **Networking Element:** Identify at least one potential networking connection on LinkedIn and draft a message to this connection, seeking advice or insight about the role or organization.

Grading Criteria:

1. **Research and Job Understanding (20%):** Evaluate the depth and relevance of the research conducted for the chosen job and how well the student understands the role and the organization.

2. **Resume Quality (30%):** Assess the clarity, organization, formatting, and relevance of the information in the resume. Check for effective use of action verbs and keywords, as well as alignment with the job requirements.

3. **Cover Letter Effectiveness (30%):** Judge the cover letter based on its ability to persuasively address the job requirements, its customization to the organization, and its overall presentation and writing quality.

4. **Networking Initiative (20%):** Rate the student's effort in identifying and reaching out to a potential networking connection, including the appropriateness and professionalism of the message drafted.

Each component should be scored individually, with feedback provided to guide the student's development in job application skills. This exercise will help students understand the nuances of applying for jobs in different sectors and the importance of tailoring their approach to each application.

Exercise for Chapter 4: Mock First Initial Interview

Background: This exercise is designed to simulate a first initial interview situation. Instructors can use this scenario to help students practice their interview skills, focusing on the STAR technique and showcasing their knowledge about the organization.

Scenario: You are a candidate for a position at XYZ Corporation, a leading firm in renewable energy solutions. The interview is conducted via Zoom by an HR Generalist, who will assess your fit for the role based on your responses, professionalism, and knowledge about the company.

Instructions for Instructors:

1. Assign a student to play the role of the interviewee.

2. As the interviewer, ask the following questions.

3. Evaluate the student's responses, focusing on their use of the STAR technique and their knowledge about XYZ Corporation.

4. Provide feedback on their performance, highlighting areas of strength and opportunities for improvement.

Sample Interview Questions:

1. **Tell me about yourself and why you are interested in working with XYZ Corporation.**

- *Expected Answer:* The student should provide a brief professional background and link their interest and skills to XYZ Corporation's focus on renewable energy.

2. **Describe a time when you had to resolve a conflict within a team using the STAR technique.**

   - *Expected Answer:* A structured response detailing a specific instance of conflict resolution, demonstrating the student's ability to navigate team dynamics effectively.

3. **XYZ Corporation prides itself on innovation. Give an example of how you have contributed to innovation in a past project or role.**

   - *Expected Answer:* The student should connect their experience with innovation to the values and objectives of XYZ Corporation.

4. **How do you stay informed about developments in the renewable energy sector?**

   - *Expected Answer:* The student should mention specific resources or practices they use to stay updated, showing their genuine interest in the industry.

5. **Recall a situation where you had to adapt to a significant change at work or in your academic environment. Use the STAR technique to describe it.**

- *Expected Answer:* A response that showcases adaptability and resilience, important traits for a dynamic industry like renewable energy.

6. **What do you know about our latest project/initiative in [specific area related to renewable energy]?**

   - *Expected Answer:* The student should show that they have done their research on XYZ Corporation's recent projects or initiatives.

7. **In your opinion, what are the biggest challenges facing the renewable energy industry today?**

   - *Expected Answer:* A thoughtful analysis of current industry challenges, reflecting the student's depth of understanding.

8. **Describe your ideal work environment and how it aligns with what you know about XYZ Corporation.**

   - *Expected Answer:* The student should link their personal work preferences with the culture and environment at XYZ Corporation.

Concluding the Interview:

- Thank the student for their time and participation.

- Discuss the key takeaways from their responses, particularly highlighting the effective use of the STAR technique.

- Offer constructive feedback, especially on how well they demonstrated knowledge about XYZ Corporation and the industry.

This mock interview scenario will help students practice their interviewing skills in a realistic setting, preparing them for actual job interviews in their field.

Exercise for Chapter 5: Identifying Quality Employers

Mock Exercise for Chapter 4: Evaluating Quality Employers

Objective: This exercise is designed to help students learn how to identify and evaluate quality employers by researching and analyzing various aspects of potential workplaces.

Scenario: Each student is tasked with selecting two companies from different sectors (e.g., a tech startup and a government agency). They will research these companies to evaluate them as potential employers based on the criteria outlined in Chapter 4.

Instructions for Instructors:

1. Divide the class into small groups or pairs.

2. Assign each group to select two companies from distinct sectors.

3. Guide students to conduct comprehensive research on each company using resources like company websites, Glassdoor, LinkedIn, Indeed, and any other relevant platforms.

4. Students should prepare a report comparing the two companies across the specified criteria.

Research and Analysis Tasks:

1. **Company Background:** Research each company's history, mission, and values.

2. **Retirement and Pension Plans:** Investigate if the companies offer pension plans or 401(k) contributions and the details of these plans.

3. **Healthcare Benefits:** Look into the healthcare plans provided, including premiums, deductibles, and coverage options.

4. **Career Growth Opportunities:** Examine opportunities for professional development and advancement within each company.

5. **Work-Life Balance:** Assess the companies' policies on PTO, remote work, and work-life balance.

6. **Company Culture:** Analyze the company culture based on employee reviews and other available data.

7. **Financial Health and Job Security:** Investigate each company's financial stability and market position.

8. **Additional Benefits:** Identify any extra benefits like tuition assistance, wellness programs, or family benefits.

Presentation: Each group will present their findings to the class, highlighting the strengths and weaknesses of each company as a potential employer.

Grading Criteria:

1. **Research Depth (30%):** Assess the thoroughness and relevance of the research conducted.

2. **Analysis and Comparison (30%):** Evaluate how well students analyzed and compared the two companies based on the outlined criteria.

3. **Presentation Quality (20%):** Judge the clarity, organization, and delivery of the presentation.

4. **Critical Thinking (20%):** Rate the students' ability to critically assess the companies and make informed judgments about their quality as employers.

Instructors should provide feedback focusing on the students' research skills, analytical thinking, and presentation abilities. This exercise will help students develop a more nuanced understanding of what makes a quality employer and how to make informed decisions about potential workplaces.

Exercise for Chapter 6: Essential Skills Beyond School Curriculum

Objective: This exercise is designed to deepen your understanding of essential life skills that extend beyond traditional academic knowledge, focusing on financial planning, communication, negotiation, work-life balance, and cultural adaptability.

Exercise Outline:

1. **Financial Planning Simulation:**

   - Task: Research and simulate a financial plan for a hypothetical career.

   - Steps: Choose a career, determine the starting salary, and project the income growth over 10 years. Using this information, create a budget that includes contributions to social security, a 401k plan, and any other savings or investment plans.

   - Reflection: Write a brief essay on the importance of understanding social security benefits, pension plans, and 401k contributions, and how these contribute to a secure financial future.

2. **Communication and Negotiation Role-Play:**

   - Task: Engage in a role-play exercise to practice communication and negotiation skills.

   - Scenario: Simulate a job offer negotiation, including salary, benefits, and other perks. One student plays the role of the job applicant, and another student or the instructor plays the role of the employer.

- Reflection: After the role-play, discuss the strategies used in the negotiation and how effective communication can impact the outcome of such negotiations.

3. **Cultural Adaptation Project:**

   - Task: Research and present on adapting to different cultural environments.

   - Steps: Select two distinct geographical locations with different cultures (e.g., a cold, rural area and a hot, urban area). Investigate the lifestyle, work environment, and cultural norms of each. Prepare a presentation on how one might adapt to working and living in these contrasting environments.

   - Reflection: Write a reflection on the importance of cultural adaptability in personal and professional life and how embracing different cultures can enrich one's experiences.

4. **Lifestyle Balance Plan:**

   - Task: Develop a personal plan for maintaining a healthy lifestyle while managing work and personal commitments.

   - Steps: Include components such as a healthy diet, exercise routine, hobbies, and time management strategies for balancing work, family, and personal time.

- Reflection: Explain how maintaining a healthy lifestyle and work-life balance contributes to both personal well-being and professional success.

Submission Requirements:

- Complete each part of the exercise and submit the required essays, presentations, and plans.

- Ensure each submission is well-organized, clear, and reflects a thoughtful understanding of the topics.

Grading Criteria:

- Depth of understanding and practical application in financial planning.

- Effectiveness in communication and negotiation role-play.

- Quality of research and presentation in cultural adaptation.

- Viability and comprehensiveness of the lifestyle balance plan.

- Clarity, organization, and insightfulness of written reflections.

Purpose of the Book

The aim of this book has been to bridge the gap between academic theory and real-world practice. It's designed to arm you with practical skills that extend beyond the classroom, preparing you for the varied challenges and opportunities in today's job market.

Encouraging Application of Knowledge

I urge you to actively apply the lessons learned here in your professional life. The true value of this book lies in its practical application, whether in enhancing communication skills, navigating financial planning, or achieving a balanced life.

The Ever-Evolving Nature of Business Communication

Business communication is a dynamic field. Embrace change and stay adaptable, as this is key to staying relevant and successful in the constantly evolving business landscape.

Final Words of Encouragement and Inspiration Never lose sight of your goals. Your journey may be fraught with challenges but remember that persistence and resilience pave the path to success. Every obstacle is an opportunity to grow and learn.

Future Prospects

Your feedback on this edition is invaluable and will inform future books and editions. I plan to delve deeper into these topics and explore new areas of growth and professional development in my subsequent works.

Thank you for your engagement and trust in this journey. Here's to a future filled with learning, success, and personal growth.

Conclusions and Remarks

As this book draws to a close, I extend my sincere thanks to you, the reader, for joining me on this educational journey. To further engage in discussions or network, feel free to connect with me on LinkedIn: linkedin.com/in/derek-bussan-33b436240.

ABOUT THE AUTHOR

Growing up in the vibrant heartland and valleys of Northeastern Iowa, I embarked on a 20 plus year academic career that began with training as an analytical chemist in my undergraduate and graduate years at the University of Iowa, Oklahoma State University, and the University of Mississippi. My journey later led me back into the halls of academia to pursue an MBA in my later years, marking a diverse career trajectory. My professional path includes postdoctoral roles at both the Oak Ridge National Laboratory and Altria, a Fortune 200 company in the tobacco industry. Additionally, I have held academic positions in chemistry at McNeese State University and Eastern Kentucky University (EKU). It was during my tenure at EKU that I recognized the need for an MBA to make a significant leap in my career. Upon completing my MBA in December 2022, I took on the role of Research Chemistry Manager at the United States Department of Agriculture and also serve as an adjunct professor in marketing at the University of North Dakota.

Made in the USA
Monee, IL
06 January 2024